PANDORA'S RUIN

Isabelle P. Byrne

Bent Key Publishing

Bent Key Publishing
Owley Wood Road, Weaverham
bentkeypublishing.co.uk

Edited by Rebecca Kenny @ Bent Key
Cover art © Samantha Sanderson-Marshall @ SMASH Design and Illustration
smashdesigns.co.uk

Printed in the UK by Mixam Ltd.

To my mother, for everything.

CONTENTS

PANDORA'S
RUIN

UNDERSTAND ME

Understand me, understand me;
I ask for nothing more —
I make it look so easy,
Yet everything's a chore.

I can play my role,
I can play yours too;
I try to close myself off,
Yet all eyes see through.

You may think you know me;
I will assure you that you do —
My mouth may say the words,
But my body tells the truth.

Understand me, understand me;
I want nothing more —
Careful now; careful now,
One step closer and
I'll shut the door.

Closed off from all the rest,
Solitude at last;
Remove all the distractions
And I'm left to face the past —

The past full of hate,
Of unsolved woe and pain,
Open the door and understand me:
I'd rather be **understood**
Than insane

⟨U⟨KOO

I'm no lead in this story; I'm just like all the rest;
I'm just another cuckoo that couldn't quite clear the nest —
I struggle just being a social contender,
My soul is lost. Time to return to sender.

Drawn to the darkness, hoping it will validate my faulty heart,
Not realising it was my mind that needed to restart:
I wasn't sure I wanted to be alive,
But my pride is fed with the need to survive.

I may have set myself on fire,
Romanticising the flowers on my pyre —
That each green laurel leaf I would earn
Was a sign of all the things I could never learn:
All I knew was I had too much rot to burn.

The Devil was my only friend,
Each fatal plan he would lend
And all the loved ones' rules I did bend,
Left with no call for help or flare to send —

And so, I accepted each tool to mend
The mind that was no longer mine,
Praying to the devil, just for a sign.

I controlled every part of my life so much,
My reality of reality was completely out of touch —

The chips in my marble body were all a mistake;
This person I had carved was just another fake,
Staring from the inside at our fragmented land,
Watching it slowly seep into the earth like sand.

All that had meaning, no longer did —
And just like the sand under my feet, I slid.
I didn't know where I wanted to be, just that it wasn't here;
That being left home alone became my greatest fear.

I was getting too tired. Too tired to get it right,
But couldn't afford to get it wrong, so I held on with all my might;
I'm such a good cheat, no one realised I had lost
Or that I kept my mouth shut, not realising the cost —

I handed over tightly-gripped reins,
Hoping the flames hadn't left a stain;
I needed help, and they agreed I did too,
And so, to solve the unanswerable, the impossible would do —

Not even they know how the electricity saves the special few,
Hoping the ions would positively ionise me all the way through;
They threw the kitchen sink in — not mentioning the toaster, too,
Now my hair is on end and I think I forgot how to chew.

Am I a magician or just another fool?
This treatment seems to be so insidiously cruel:
To strap me down and shock me surely isn't a rule.

This was the room I entered with pure lunacy
Where somehow, I'd agreed to be shocked with electricity,
Because I didn't fit within the acceptability of society.

I wanted nothing more
Than not to feel that inner shredder any more,
So I walked toward the sign that read *ECT* above the door —

And so they turned the lights on up inside my head —
They even checked if anyone was at home: alive or dead
But when I woke, the world became just a sea of static,
My head and dread ceased to be overly erratic...
And now? I'm alone, floating in this sea of static.

I'm alive without reason or needing to know
Although my memory is now a little touch and go,
They saved my mind in exchange for my soul —
But what's the mind with no soul at all?

THE MINOTAUR

Follow me, follow me, she eagerly said
But as she turned, the minotaur horns protruded from her head

As Pandora closed the box after releasing all human ills
She sat in sickness and swallowed her pills

She punished herself from that day on
Deceptive expectation replaced hope
And finally, hope was gone —

Pandora, Pandora: what did you do?
You opened the box in the hope of finding truth:
Instead, the demons, darkness and all things cruel
Now swirl around you, using pessimism as fuel —

I tackle the maze, each wall an exhibit of a painful past;
Why is it the good memories fade but the trauma lasts?

This is where you reside in darkness, whether it's known or not —
You buried yourself within a maze in the hope of being forgot,

The twists and turns, bricks and mortar
Each well-rehearsed verse that does well to deceive,
You are so learnt in dissociation
Yet always surprised when another leaves —

Pandora! Pandora!
If you begin to cry then your deceit will show,
Your worst fear isn't of doing wrong but letting people know

On the final corner I turn, I'm met with a wave of tears:
All have been locked up and stored, one for each of my fears,

Down comes the water, but not in drips and drops —
Instead, a *force majeure*, that once it starts — never stops

The trick to living is let the water rise to the top
As there is never any point fighting a force that cannot be stopped

I'm dragged from the surface and sink quickly down
There, I see my will for life fighting not to drown —
How do you beat a maze that was made not to be solved?
I can't bear to watch this last bit of logic get dissolved

It wasn't the tears that drowned me, but the silence in my head;
If honesty was the only option? I'd sooner wish to be dead
What once was a space of safety all alone in this cave,
I realise in order for me to live any life... I need to be **brave**

To go back down every concrete corridor I have duly made
In the hope that with acceptance, these dark thoughts will fade —
I may never stop crying for myself in many ways,
But it's worth fighting for so I can at least

Enjoy the good days.

THE LAND

I swam from the land
Out and out into the sea;
As I turned around,
It had sunk far beneath me.

I did not need this land,
Just the security it brought —
It let me swim without worry;
Now, every kick is heavy with thought.

The waves lap my body and as I begin to slow,
The thought of that land and the familiar does grow.

The more I think, the more I drown —
Filled to the top with sand,
All in the hope of finding
That sweet piece of land,

As I sink down, down, down
Into the ambiguous abyss,
I search the sea-bed for that land of happiness;
I soon find that I still have the strength to swim.
I always did — but sometimes, the brain is the weakest limb

The limb that can make your whole body lame.
Look to the past — the land —
Just something to blame;

But I will continue to swim
And empty my pockets of sand
And with this —
I shall build my own piece of land.

MY ROLE

My eyes are seething.
Overwhelmed with liquid sorrow
I imprison them inside,
Wishing for a brighter tomorrow —

I catch my breath again.
Short... sharp... sip... *inhale.*
My heart is in pure panic;
My body wounded and frail,

A hard and heavy smile
My worst performance of the year;
As optimistic as I try,
My mind is more far than near.

My hollow, howling heart
Pounds at every thought;
I try, retry and try, yet
I am always falling short.

I am not the actress
I once used to be;
No script or play to follow;
I have trouble just playing *me.*

SHATTERPROOF RULER

Like a shatterproof ruler
It breaks just the same;
We all have our flaws
Yet we use a different name;

To bring back the pieces
Shattered amongst the rest,
Glue all the shards together;
I'll never feel my best.

I snap under pressure —
The cracks begin to show;
Like my old school ruler,
I close my eyes before the blow;

I will be moulded again
With the old and the new;
Just waiting to break
And tear through the glue —

With my shape regained,
No one will ever tell
That once I was shattered,
And into pieces I had fell.

SCRUB

A tidy house; a tidy mind.
I scrub, wash, bleach
In the hope to find
Just one thing to clear my mind;

I can clean the house
But it just won't help;
What else to do but
Scream or yelp?

Scrub as I may,
My skin is dirtier than before.
I am a mess upon
The tidiest floor;

Oh, how I cover myself
With sores
As if to mark out
Scores and scores,

A tick chart
That's nearly filled,
On the wish to defeat
A disease that can't be killed:

I can clean all I wish
But I will never feel new,
No one can help —
Not me, not him, not you.

NUMB

All I am is numb —
What goes up
must come down.
My smile is swapped
for another frown;

I can't be high,
Nor can I be low —
All that I am
is what I choose to show.

I cannot wait to go up and up;
for the water to fall
in my half empty cup —

For the sun to shine
and the flowers to bloom,
I need a sweet escape
to my dark, dank gloom

To be above the clouds
far and high;
to stop my thoughts and
silence my cry —

It will come again.
I will catch my breath.
I will feel the warm,
Not feel like death.

When I am there
I will take it in stride;
that even through sadness,
I still have my pride.

I got to the end,
the battle, I won —
And I will be graced
like a flower in the sun.

THE MAGIC

Change, for me, is not fun.
It tears at the ligaments of my matter and
My front stage, and
This is when I shatter —

The pieces, they fall.
How do pieces put together pieces?
Well, that is what magic is for —

One in the morning, then two more.
Then: a little anxiety, nausea, and
That's not all —
But oh! The magic is dark.
It tackles the broken
By breaking its fall,

And oh, I see why it steals your soul —
To save the mind... but
What is the mind with no soul at all?

ALL OF A SUDDEN

Heavy eyes that won't close,
I try to sleep: a nap or doze
But it just won't work.
I'm broken I suppose;
Is this really the life I chose?

Not a life at all,
One step, two step — then a fall.
Maybe it is best if I just crawl?
Yes. I shall crawl. And crawl. And crawl.

Hands are bleeding. Knees are torn;
I guess I never had time to mourn
Yet I think, from eve to dawn —
Every shout, scream and scorn,

I repeat and emphasise
All the looks and lies;
I feel swamped by flies
Crawling into my mind through my eyes;

Why care at all over such small things?
I have no choice when the doorbell rings;
It sings and sings!

And this is all my fault.
A part of me, like a screw and a bolt,
But then why does it feel like a wound with salt?

My mind spins.
I'm waiting for it to
Halt

INTO THE DARKNESS

A feeling so dark
No light is seen.
So dark; darker than
It has ever been

No stars to shake it
No sun or spark;
It can't be lit
When it's pitch-black dark

A pit of self-distress
And no-one to save me;
When I'm this lost in this darkness
With only melancholy
To caress —

If only it were harmless —

Swallowed up whole
Without a thought;
I'm digested like any other.
It's taking me just like it took
My mother's mother —

A tablet, a few, or many:
How many, how many,

How many
Before the light comes?
If it comes. Will it come?
It's not coming!

No light to this darkness,
Just me, myself,
My darkest!

SIT AND THINK

I find time to think and ponder
On things and thoughts and
Sorts-of-thoughts to be thought about:
The circle, the figure of eight.

Trapped upon, inside, around
In a round-about way;
To-and-fro
Like a game of *Catch* without the throw.

I will sit and scribble, thinking
That what I say has meaning;
This is not true!

I write to write
Just how I think to think —
I have no choice but to
Continue the cycle;

Today. Tomorrow. The day before —
Shall I learn or stall;
Succeed or fall?
I do not know —

As I learn and learn and learn,
All I have learned is this:
I have learned little to nothing at all.

Nothing to write home.
Nothing to write but
Write what comes from the ink,
Directed by a head
That has no direction.
No direction. **No direction**

I'm so tired of trying to live with
Someone I do not know —
Who I will *never* know and
If anything, that is all
I know of myself.

It is my right to write, they say —
But rather not a right to write,
But the right to be read and be criticised;

Read as the girl with nothing to write
But a life of nothing. Woes of nothing,
Some troubles of nothing —
All worth less than ink!

DΞΛTH

Gluttony. Greed. Sin.
Any day now, you'll meet him —
In the dark he will wait;
No point in planning an escape —
Just a dark fate that we all will face.
Every creed, colour and race —
Are you ready for the end,
Or even the start?
It only takes something small
To stop the heart.
A cold touch of the hand,
Then comes the dust and sand;
Drowned forever under the earth.
Hoping and waiting for a second birth,
Crawling in our skin
As we head for nothing but a bleak, wooden bin.

RIVER STYX

I've always felt stuck in the River Styx.
Dragged below the tides into the swell of souls' weighted kicks,
hoping to reach the surface
but their hands wrap around my ankles,
anchoring me in place.

Stuck in the River Styx
with Charon's paddle, wading through the lost:
too late to pray; too late to pay my way
to something better.
Each breath rolls from my lips
as if to escape for itself.

Motionless, with wings sodden, wet;
wings that weren't made for water, and
now, heavy pillows are weightily attached to my back.

Stuck in the River Styx,
the faces of pain and anguish are just whirling,
waiting to be extinguished,
but the water won't help put out the fire
like you thought it would.
Instead, it suspends you in the salt:

Forever stuck in the River Styx,
The ferryman sails so easily above us all:
to and fro. For those that pay and for those that can't,
just lay within
The River Styx.

LACKADAISICAL HEAD

Who's gonna save her when she's already dead
Two braids wrapped around her lackadaisical head?

Paint-dipped sleeves hold on to your sawdust hands
Under shady trees and shaky lands,

She stares up unto the twinkling between the green
Wondering if she'll remember what she's seen
Or when or what it even means —

Some get to be the trunk, while the rest are just leaves
Unless she is to deceive with the mighty webs she weaves.

Her tongue is out, ready to catch the tears,
Big, glazed eyes fit for doe and deer;

Tears fill her half-empty glass:
One moment she's down, the next: it's passed.

Looking up through clouded eyes,
She tells herself that love always dies.
She's electric: every touch a shock,
Jump the fence and try the lock,
Unfazed and crazed, inside her own maze,
Sadness just a haze that she blazes away
Hoping to be asked to stay.

She's just washed-up goods,
Fighting to find herself amongst the woods.

Let the blossom fall,
From the branches so tall,
Hunting that rustling call:

She's just washed-up goods;
Keeps drifting on down.

The Boatman has been paid;
She paid Charon with kisses as trade,
Floating along in a wooden coffin she'd made:
At the bow of the boat, the boatman stood
Drifting down the river, just as Ophelia did,
Meeting her fate and finally meeting King ID:

So drift, drift like the blossom and leaves
Down the midnight river into stormy seas,
So she drifts... drifting on by, ready to meet her fate:
Come As You Are written above the gate .

She was made for pain
Comforted by a heavy chain
And by the pouring rain
In the hope to wash away
The sadness in her brain.

I OUGHT

I thought I had to be OK,
That it shouldn't matter what they say;
I would just smile and hold the tears away.

I thought I had to be so brave
When my hair began to fall to its grave;

That starting school with no hair
Was better than not being there —

I thought I had to hold back fear;
But when my mother got ill, it notched up a gear.

I thought I had to carry on,
That the worst had come and the worst had gone —
But it just. Kept. Coming.

I thought I had to be smart
(I always knew I'd fall short on that part)
But it wasn't 'til I was seven did my reading start,
And they never knew.

I thought I had to hide the whole of me
Because I was none of what I thought I was allowed to be:

I thought I should make people laugh;
Even at five I had all these stories I'd craft,

I was addicted to creating happy tears,
The type that distract from the joker's fears —

I thought I had to get it right,
That everything I did wrong
Was another sleepless night,

Now I'm so lost
I don't know what to think —
Thinking of what I ought to have thought
Has me at my brink;
But that's something
I ought
Not
To
Think.

ᛖNOUᚷH

Just like that, being human wasn't allowed.
I know I preach on what to be, and how, out loud
And I expect so little from those who ask too much:
I can hug and kiss and with each touch —
It just isn't enough, so I hold on with my tightest clutch;
I know now that I will never be enough; my love just isn't enough,
Having to prove myself to you is just too tough.
I don't know how to defend who I am
When I know what I am, and I feel like just another social scam —
I know you feel duped into loving me
Because I am not who you thought I'd be;
I'm not a religious type, but there is *one* biblical line
That always seems relevant in this life of mine:
You're so quick to spot the speck in my eye,
But blinded by the beam in your own, which you let lie —
It doesn't matter what I say;
You'd just turn and look the other way.
You think my tears are here to deceive;
It doesn't matter what I say for you to believe
That I'm just too tired to be someone new —
If I'm not good enough, then I'll accept the truth
But you invested yourself too early, you see:
And when the light turns to darkness, you lose sight of me.
I suffer in silence behind big smiles and canned laughter,
When all I was looking for was a *happily ever after*
Yet I smoke so many cigarettes and drink so much caffeine
That when it comes to loving someone, they aren't too keen
And I end up unseen:
The reason I have become so resistant to change
Is the knowledge that I'm just really fucking strange.
That's not enough and it never will be;
I can't stand to lie or push the good parts of me.
It's just another voice adding harmony to my own misery.

I eat too much. Smoke too much. Talk too much. Fuck too much.
Each one an irrational crutch:
The crutch that gave me control when I had none
And now you call for all of them to be gone —
But it isn't as easy as putting out the smoke,
Or the fear of eating too loudly, so I'm stuck in a silent choke;
I don't want to defend the way I cope
Because I just want to sit and let the smoke bring the hope,
Because right now the only thing working is the dope.
I'm beaten and bruised and feeling the heat;
I fall to my knees and suck the blood from my teeth,
Looking down at his hoofed feet —
This is not the end and this is not another defeat.
So I smile like the sinner I am;
Sorry you must have mistaken me
With someone who gives a damn!
God might have been my potter but the Devil was the man —
The man who cast me in fire to make me hard,
So these little cogs aren't that easy to discard
And although God has come to meet me,
The Devil's with me all the time, you see.
And if it wasn't for him, then I'd struggle to be free,
Free of the rules that I am supposed to meet
In the hope I will use them as a tool to defeat,
Defeat the illness that makes me a social cheat —
Because when you are faced with darkness,
You have to become the darkest;
You have to become the Devil to rid away the evil.
It is far better to be hoofed than winged
When you live a life where your limbs are stringed,
Whether it is the doctors, the therapists — even you:
How the fuck can you give advice on what to do?

So enough is enough.

I don't want to play the game any more;
I've been beaten on both sides and I've lost score.
So please — I need no more. No more;
I'm on my knees and I'm begging for you to just not say
The things that you are about to say.
I already know my weaknesses and know you do, too;
So please don't act like this is an attack on you.
These little evils that I have kept around
Have been the only thing I can call solid ground
And if you cannot see how ingrained these evils might be,
Then I can't afford for you to get it wrong with me.
You can't ask someone to compromise with such rigidity.
So please, I beg for you to turn on the light,
To understand my long lived fight —
So please, see me. I mean, really *see me*,
See the girl that is too scared to show herself completely.

TELL ME WHAT I NEED NEVER HEAR

Your words became just another voice in my head,
but this time round I have the strength not to wish to be dead.
I have learned that it's not a sin to be who I am:
I am honest with you, but you didn't wish to give a damn.

Why? Tell me what I already know;
just inform me of the weaknesses I show
as you tell me that I'm no good at driving,
that smoking 20-a-day isn't surviving,
that I am not that good at sailing,
that the only thing I'm actually good at — is failing.
That when I'm excited, I can't keep my voice down,
that I can't make a decision whether to float or drown,
that I'm either talking too much or not at all,
not taking recovery seriously when I'm on my knees to crawl —

Blaming it on my *self-destructive* behaviour is a fictitious failure,
too negative to even discuss what I know
because you are too weak to listen to another woe:
You'd rather bury your head and make me go.

My tears of pain and desperation are claimed to be a tactic
when all I know is, it's the guilt that makes you so erratic;

You tell me to shower and that I'm dirty,
while you are so consumed
that you are struggling just being thirty.

Every smoke of every cig was twenty digs a day,
my car smells of smoke (which you can't help but say),

Punished for not being intimate with you,
but unable to kiss you because you don't allow me to.

My hands are too dry for me to even touch you;
I taste bad; my smell disgusts and repels the love we grew.
You left me to cry on my own and unable to breathe
because you can't help but think it's a move to deceive —

You don't want to believe this anguish comes from your words,
and so my lips are sewn shut and the silence makes you worse:
I just can't think of what to say to converse —

I know now you envy that I could see straight through
when you struggled to see my pain and my truth;
but you never could see me — not even a little,
and so instead you sit in your own world, where you whittle —

I excused your ignorance and doubted my own head
I really did love you; losing you was what I'd dread —
but like you said, I'm only good for the music and the sex,
and anything more was just *too complex* —

How can I get through to you?
I can't laugh or cry or plead with you
to do the things I need you to do —

I'm sat, exhausted, hoping you'll eventually see my side,
because right now it's like the blind leading the blind;

You had enough energy to lend me some,
and I gave you so much I became totally numb.

So goodbye the lover that showed me I needed to be more,
that my life was not meant to be mine and yours:
No. My life is mine and I choose to live,
and all the digs you gave won't stop my need to give.

I really wanted you to love me right,
but that was never going to happen with your refusal to fight;
with each fight you got further away from the truth,
the truth — that loving you felt like an ache from a loose tooth

As much as I wait for you to get it right,
I know you never will be able to have me in your sight
because it's all about you, blinded by your own plight —
you haven't got the time or the patience for me,
and that's OK. I understand it completely,
but you should have let me go so I could save the rest of me,
because now — now, you've beaten away my positivity,

And I'm going through trauma therapy.
Yet you think this is a good time for you to be hard on me?
If we refuse to look at the pain in another's eyes,
then we become further from solving our own fucking lies.

Being spun into my own web can be hard for my loved ones to see,
you change the narrative around me,
that somehow I am the one who never wanted to be free —
you met me with the deepest distain,
whilst I was suffering from this disease of pain.

Watching me suffocate; that's what you thought I deserved,
and even when I asked for help, you didn't have the nerve.

If it's not me, it's you — and that can't be true for you;
you only have enough pity for yourself, you're the person who,
guilty through omission, decided to do nothing —
when all I needed was for you
to do something.

HIM

Do as I say and not as I do
He bellows from above;
You aren't here to show your compassion
and especially not your love.
Oh no — you have to follow my *rules in life*
And you have to feel the pain and strife!

We must jump through his hoops and play by his rules;
we must never question him or the way he blames his tools —
Finding purpose in things that are purposeless,
just another of his carrot-less mules.
He tweaks his 'tache as he plans his next move;
what do I need to do? What do I need to prove?
How many more magpies do I need to salute?
How many times do I need to fail for it to compute
that you can't be the master of my life without a dispute?

Whether you're the man in the sky or the man at the top,
I don't really know you well enough for me to be your prop;
I don't claim to be a Marxist — well, not as such,
but I feel like I'm the proletariat and you are out of touch.
I'm strung to all these rules that are hung up in our history,
and they are so out-of-date and completely contradictory —
It's no wonder our society is so wound up in conspiracy.

I'd much prefer to lay on a thousand hot coals
than listen to how I should do as I'm told.

I can feel your breath on my neck and your gun to my head,
so I call your bluff, wishing you to dare me to be dead.
I'm sick of being just another goose to be force-fed;
there isn't anything you can say or that should have been said.

So I threw myself to the ground and turned and fled;
I'd rather be a goat than another sheep to be led.

I run as far as I can, towards fire burning red;
The Devil welcomes me home and back into his bed —
at least I will be punished for who I am, not who I should be.
I feel at home in Hell with his hooves around me.

Because here, everyone is just who they want to be —
to be who they are
without apology.

THE BETTER OF TWO EVILS

Nihilist. Hedonist. The better of two evils
While he sits above me, sticking in his needles

Convinced there is something dark inside of me
That negatively ionises those in close proximity

I suffocated the angel on the opposing shoulder
With my ego's reflections in the eye of the beholder

The only evil I continue to have within me
Is the obsessive wish to make everything easy

But by accepting all those traits you hate
I tore down your rusted-shut flood gates

Whilst I accept every trait you wish to be gone
You can't understand how I could do that to someone

How could I like the parts you hate?
You think I'm just encouraging your current state

Without the wish for you to change and better who you are
Beating yourself is not conducive to getting far

You think the only way to be free of the constraints
Is to fall to your knees and beg to the saints

Your need to be stronger and faster than you really are
Is just you — reopening each and every scar

The scars planted by the ones you loved
Yet we may never understand what we call our blood

And so you wish not to treat yourself with any kindness
As those bruises are far from behind us

You believe that to be a form of weakness
As a life of beatings comes with a form of completeness

Instead you beat yourself with the same stick they did.
You render yourself back to being that scared little kid.

Because there is comfort in knowing you aren't enough
That the road was always meant to be this tough

And so you tell me that you think I need to be punished to succeed
When all it is, is more love that I need

Nurture yourself the way you should have always done
Whether it be by you, or a strange someone

Because you won't get too far
When you keep moving your bar

To keep to the words of the angel inside your head
And yet it's the same angel that fills you with constant dread

The rules are a lot tougher when you want to be right
Forever crawling to the finish line that's out of sight

Yet I sit with the Devil who allows you to get it wrong
And become comfortable knowing I'd have lost all along

And so it takes away the importance of getting it right
That this life was hard enough even before you joined the fight.

The fight within yourself to be the best of who you are
So there is no need to constantly feel under par

When in fact it is the Devil who allows you to fail and succeed
He takes your hand in his hoof and begins to proceed
To his fired-up world where he sits and stokes the freed.

I changed the rules because those I was given don't make sense
Having to live my life under false pretence

And life is unfair and no one follows the same rules
So I grabbed my pitchfork so as not to be a fool

And I turned the rules right back around
So I could have a chance in the second round

That these rules that bring purpose to your head
Don't hold the same meaning when I've spent my life in dread

Dread that I might get it wrong
If I were Christian, I'd be punished for not singing the same song

That the constraints that I felt so early on
Mean nothing to me, now; I banish them to be gone

I can't live a life where there is a right and wrong
When I know the wrong was right all along

So don't punish me for not holding the same ethos in life
Life can't be lived with your back against his knife

The reason I follow the pleasure is to paint over my pain
I don't need any more beating to achieve my aim

I need to know that it's OK to do the opposite of what you do
Because I follow the rules of the Devil, not you

Never to suppress another's way to cope
Because you might follow the angel but the Devil brings me hope

So forgive those who don't act like you
Don't expect them to do as you do

Understand that each person had to learn what works for them
When it doesn't match yours, there's no reason to condemn

Patience comes easier when you know life is hard
When you're friends with an angel, forgiveness is easier to discard

Because we think that our wrongs make us weak
When in fact it's the right way that's impossible to seek —

But when you know you're going to Hell
It isn't so bleak.

PANDORA'S RUIN

Pandora, Pandora; you never had a chance on this deceptive earth.
Damned to duty and bound by the stars at birth,
Gilded together with the gods' golden ink,
An invisible chain soldered with each link —
Stirred into a godly cocktail of venom and honey,
White hair radiating the light when it got sunny,
Wrapped in a robe of beauty that uncomfortably fit,
The fruit of life that came from Zeus' pit —
Made as a weapon, disarming the gods to empower humanity,
Not knowing her story was set to end so tragically;
A gift and a giver. Turn the seas to syrup to slow down man,
Her femme fatale was something else to ban —
The gift of all gifts, the ultimate portrayal of human,
That her body was godly but all else was an illusion.
Purposefully flawed to fail
As even the softest ember can cause a fire;
Without knowing, Pandora continued to feed her desire,
Thick thighs and hollow eyes, pomegranate heart
Set for ruin from the very start —
Serpent-laced veins roaming under marble skin,
Untameable in sight of her next inevitable sin;
Spitting out pits from the cherries that stained her lips.
Always dirty from digging her own grave;
Death wasn't something she feared, but braved —

It didn't matter what each god had brought,
She was a human led by afterthought:
A likeable sinner softened with naivety,
She was a hot mess and a liability,
A likeness to Eve, you may have thought —
But she was the forbidden fruit that the Devil brought
With apple juice dripping through her dreams,
As her mind's plumpness pressed against its seams

They insisted on resisting life's pleasures,
Not understanding her needs' true measures —

Little did they know that with each human there's always ID;
Pandora's pleasure impulse was something she always hid,
Until the day came that she would open that lid —

She needed to feed her need to know her impulse
To fulfil her desires and distract from the pain,
Wishing what's next might settle her brain;
Barefoot on a path of fallen laurels,
Forbidden fruits and broken morals —
Snapping the stems of the agapanthus with her fingertips,
With a deep hunger, she started to lick her lips,

Serpents squirmed across branches overhead
In anticipation of the chaos ahead —
The serpent sang to her in several tongues
That sinning could help right her wrongs.

An unquenchable hunger for happiness
Meant she had to perfect her craftiness;
She ignores all the rationality she had been taught —
She opened that box in curiosity, not knowing she'd be caught.

Pandora's pleasure impulse was set to *on*,
Before she could close the box, the ills had left and gone —

Like smoke, the evil of this world seeped from the box,
Weaving through her golden locks;
A runaway locomotive took to her spine
As the serpents watched her from their vine —

The devil took his seat on top of splintered ribs,
Lighting all 20 of his *Superking* cigs;
A storm of unsettled souls swimming through her bones,
Ears bleeding as the world lets out deafening groans —
She had given the world the punishment Zeus intended,
Not realising all the fruits she'd eaten were fermented.

Her greed had a diet of secrecy and so this time she was left hollow,
As all the ills of world began to follow;
She had bitten more of the apple than she could swallow
Spending her life so hard to mend it,
And now she had thoughts on how to end it.

Blamed for being a pawn in the gods' game,
The only human on Earth that they could blame;
Living her life with the weight of another's guilt and shame.
The creator of its content never got convicted
And so Pandora received a life sentence, just as Zeus had wished it.
But — there *was* one thing that settled her mind,
That Hope was left in the box as she shut it just in time,
Haunted by sickness, loneliness and the presence of death,
Hoping her next might be her last breath —
So she ran, as fast as she could, to the river
With each PTSD flashback she would shiver;
Snapping the ivy that contained her flesh,
Pulling its tentacle veins from her own.
Her slyness? Not so sly, and her secrets known,
That she succumbed to being a human that wished not to be alone.
Tussling through the rye, avoiding the inevitable trial,
Before she looked behind her, she had reached the Nile.

Pandora was forever punished for breaking the rules
She never wanted to follow,

Plagued with darkness and a curse of sorrow
So she dove into the water to cleanse her soul
With happiness as her only goal —
Finally bare, but not unscathed from the ride,
Her tears rolled out with the lull of the tide;
Weighted by all of God's rules, which she had to abide,
Feeling the power of the stars that bound her,
But it was through sin that she finally found her —
Another fallen angel who never got their wings
As each force of nature has their own song to sing,
Why punish human nature for what they've always been:
Vessels of gluttony and vessels of sin?

These expectations that the stars instil
Will never be stronger than our human will.
Pandora questioned these godly expectations
And broke them still.

Never to contort into a sort that was wished for,
Constantly looking for the answers and more,
If anything, Pandora's defiance did show
That it's never a sin to dare to know.

Sapere Aude

ARISTOTLE, WHAT DO YOU SEE?

Aristotle, do you like what you see?
Changing our virtue-less world into a democracy;

What do we do to make your words true?
The leaders of the world are only helping a few;

Where is our knowledge, or even our virtue?
Are we really civilised knowing less than we once knew?

We have policies made by politicians and MPs;
bias and perspective is our new plague of disease.

It's not that our leaders don't mean us well
but their prerogative is in trade and what we can sell —

We have poverty, hunger and those without nation states
refusing food, shelter and human rights at our gates;

I want to believe that we can all do so much more
yet the media feeds our fears and adds another lock to our door.

People are people; we never chose our birth-place;
we shouldn't be handcuffing people and stating a case,

Are we only humans when we have citizenship
within boundaries and walls?
We need change and so we wait
for the crow from the Cock of Gaul.

EL TORO

El Toro, El Toro, looking at me,
stuck in the fatal fight on the wish to be free,

Dead palms and ivory horns used to amuse,
just some more life for the amphitheatre architect to abuse,

Thrown into the middle of the circle once more,
as I pick myself up off the sand-covered floor
and throw the anxiety out of my clammy hands —
I glance up at all those I've tried to prove wrong
sitting in the stands,

My *Lady of Guadalupe* hanging around my neck
(holding on to faith always kept my mind in check)
but this time? I called for all hands on deck.

As I tip my hat, he tips his horns,
ready to be crowned with a crown of thorns.

As I begin to wave the Muleta at his feet,
I'd have to move fast for me to have a chance to defeat —
his brow lowered and his eyes flickering red;
his hooves shifting the sand to steady his tread,

The heat wavering above the sand —
this was supposed to be my final stand.
The sand was blistering my bare-footed soles,
but **nothing** compared to the Devil-stoked coals.
I guess he saw the red within me;
I turned to slow without a chance to flee.

A dance to the death I could never win;
and now? I'm to be judged for every lived sin:

Every sin I ever committed,
every time I swore, every tooth I gritted;
buried in my own bloodied grit.
Punished for the life that I just didn't fit —

This wasn't going to be the last fight I fought,
nor the last big fish to be caught;
my fate was sealed with God's passing thought
that this bull was never to stop; it went on red.
Deaf to my pleas of not wanting to be dead
but it wouldn't matter how far I had fled —
this bull was what the Devil had bred.

As I swirled on my heels, meeting the beast's eyes,
I realised that we had both been fed the same lies:
that in reality, neither one of us had to die,
but our lives weren't something that we could buy.
We had to follow the rules. To compromise.

So it was just me and him, and him and me;
neither had a choice to be truly free,
so we look to the same man to let us be —
not knowing God and the Devil grew on the same tree.

Each apple we ate was one step further from the gate
and it wasn't love we were here for, but rather to hate.

And just like that: in two I was torn,
the victor with a crown between two blood-stained horns
and the blood coagulating into the ground beneath;
the ringing of the devil sharpening his sheath:
I was too soon to belong to another beast —
no lord or saviour, not even a priest:

Cheers of joy drown out my suffocated cries,
I still have a wish to be seen — even in my demise.

God made the beast to live amongst mankind,
but now I see that He created *me* with him in mind.

ACKNOWLEDGEMENTS

To all of those who have suffered.

To all of those who stood by their side.

To all of the poets who have supported my journey.

To Andy and Amanda for being the first welcoming faces in the Mancunian poetry scene.

To Bent Key and Smash Design & Illustration for transforming my work into something beautiful.

To Mrs T J Ray.

To Manolo, Vangelis and Zygmunt.

To my sisters.

ABOUT THE AUTHOR

Isabelle Pandora Byrne is a Mancunian poet. She has had a life filled with misfortune in terms of her health and her work focuses on her mental health journey. She has studied in Nottingham and Manchester with an in-depth knowledge of social frameworks and social ills.

Isabelle's work is a raw expression of what it is to live with mental illness, treatment and recovery. After her stay in psychiatric care, she began to work on Mental Health wards whilst studying Counselling and Psychotherapy and, later, International Development. She currently works within the NHS as a Phlebotomist.

Isabelle's written work looks to create better narratives for those who feel outcast from society. Isabelle is also a mixed-media artist who enjoys creating poetry shorts accompanied by her music.

She is a cinephile and enjoys her coffee with a smoke.

ABOUT BENT KEY

It started with a key.

Bent Key is named after the bent front-door key that Rebecca Kenny found in her pocket after arriving home from hospital following her car crash. It is a symbol of change, new starts, risk and taking a chance on the unknown.

Bent Key is a micropublisher with ethics. We do not charge for submissions, we do not charge to publish and we make space for writers who may struggle to access traditional publishing houses, specifically writers who are neuro-divergent or otherwise marginalised. We never ask anyone to write for free, and we like to champion authentic voices.

All of our beautiful covers are designed by our graphic designer Sam at SMASH Design & Illustration, a graphic design company based in Southport, Merseyside.

Find us online:
bentkeypublishing.co.uk

Instagram & Facebook   @bentkeypublishing
Twitter   @bentkeypublish

If you have found yourself affected by any of the topics covered in this collection, please refer to these resources for help and assistance:

SANEline   **4.30pm-10.30pm every day**
If you're experiencing a mental health problem or supporting someone else, you can call SANEline on 0300 304 7000

National Suicide Prevention Helpline UK   **24/7 service**
Offers a supportive listening service to anyone with thoughts of suicide. You can call the National Suicide Prevention Helpline UK on 0800 689 5652

Shout   **24/7 service**
If you would prefer not to talk but want some mental health support, text SHOUT to 85258. Shout offers a completely confidential text service providing support if you are in crisis and need immediate help

Papyrus HOPELINEUK
Weekdays 10am-10pm / weekends 2-10pm / bank hols 2-10pm
If you're under 35 and struggling with suicidal feelings, or concerned about a young person who might be struggling, you can call Papyrus HOPELINE on 0800 0684141 email pat@papyrus.uk.org or text 07786 209697.

Switchboard   **10am–10pm every day**
If you identify as gay, lesbian, bisexual or transgender, you can call Switchboard on 0300 330 0630 , email chris@switchboard.lgbt or use their webchat service. All phone operators identify as LGBT+.

Scan here to access information about urgent mental health support from the NHS in England